The A-Men
Rethinking Autism
By
Jack Gunthridge

The A-Men: Rethinking Autism
By
Jack Gunthridge

Introduction

I grew up not knowing I was autistic. When I was finally diagnosed, it didn't really change anything. It gave me some understanding of the things I went through in life. And if you ask me why it didn't change anything, I guess I would have to answer with, "Because I grew up with the Muppets and watching science fiction and movies about superheroes."

The Muppets taught me it was okay to be my own kind of different and that it was okay to have my own dreams, even if only I believed in it. It was still my dream, and maybe I could get a few more people to believe in it until it became several other people's dream, too.

Science fiction and shows about superheroes taught me that the people who grow up different often end up with a skill that helps to save the world. It was what made them get made fun of as a child, but they persevered and developed their skill. What made them different was actually something to be celebrated. It just took time for the world to recognize that.

I might get in trouble for this essay because I would rather see autism as an advantage instead of a disability or a disease. I admit to struggles in my life, but it is too easy to focus on what we haven't achieved in life. What I have learned about successful autistic people in history is that they had a positive attitude.

It is generally accepted that Albert Einstein would be on the autism spectrum if he had been born today. All we can do now is look at his behavior and say he exhibited autistic tendencies. Paul Coelho listed these ten life lessons from Einstein.

1. **Follow Your Curiosity** "I have no special talent. I am only passionately curious."

2. **Perseverance is Priceless** "It's not that I'm so smart; it's just that I stay with problems longer."

3. **Focus on the Present** "Any man who can drive safely while kissing a pretty girl is simply not giving the kiss the attention it deserves."

4. **The Imagination is Powerful** "Imagination is everything. It is the preview of life's coming attractions. Imagination is more important than knowledge."

5. **Make Mistakes** "A person who never made a mistake never tried anything new."

6. **Live in the Moment** "I never think of the future – it comes soon enough."

7. **Create Value** "Strive not to be a success, but rather to be of value."

8. **Don't be repetitive** "Insanity: doing the same thing over and over again and expecting different results."

9. **Knowledge Comes From Experience** "Information is not knowledge. The only source of knowledge is experience."

10. **Learn the Rules and Then Play Better** "You have to learn the rules of the game. And then you have to play better than anyone else."

Jim Henson, another person suspected of being on the spectrum, is quoted as saying, "I believe we form our own lives, that we create our own reality, and that everything works out for the best. I know I drive some people crazy with what seems to be ridiculous optimism, but it has always worked out for me."

I see too many people trapped in a mentality thinking they can't do something. When I first started self-publishing my books, I had writer friends who weren't going to follow my lead. They were going to be legitimate writers and wait to be accepted by publishers. They haven't published anything. I publish whatever I want, get letters from fans, have people in college writing final papers on my works, have kids in high school doing projects on my books, and get fan mail from people around the world.

Sure, I'm not a legitimate author in the sense of Stephen King, but I'm making some money and have people that like my work. That is all I have ever really wanted for my work. In fact, I would take the fan mail over money, except that I do need the money to live. I'm not going to argue with people who want to pay me for doing something I love.

In the same way, I don't see my autism as a limitation or a disability. Not to criticize people, but I don't believe in the pity party people throw themselves because they aren't where they want to be in life. I'm not successful because… And you can enter however you see yourself into that spot. It doesn't have to be autism. It could be a woman, homosexual, or a minority. Whatever it is, you are shaping your perspective to equate unhappiness with something you essentially are.

Look at Jim Henson's quote or Einstein's rules. We create our own reality. You are creating a reality of failure based on race, gender, sexuality, or disability. Do you expect somebody to hire you when you are projecting that to them. You are surrounding yourself with negativity, which the person you are interviewing with is going to be picking up on.

Don't be bitter because you didn't get a job, use it as a learning experience. Einstein's rules of trying something new and staying with a problem. I have learned more by not succeeding than I would have ever learned if I had been successful. Learning the rules means I have to look at what I did that was good, examine what I did that didn't work, and see what I can learn from it. Successful people never have a victim mentality.

When I first found out I was autistic, I had some friends and co-workers say, "I'm sorry" when I told them about it. I never understood this. Why should you be sorry? It doesn't change anything. It does allow me to look at my life and to understand the things I have trouble with. It lets me change my perspective and to understand that I need help from time to time and that I don't need to be ashamed for asking for that help. It doesn't make me less of a person because I have sensory issues of don't quite understand social settings.

I don't see autism as a disability or a disease. It's not a life sentence. My life isn't going to end because I'm autistic. I can have people tell me I can't do something because of it, but I just point out there are things they can't do. We are all disabled to some degree. Can you write a song? Paint a masterpiece that will hang in a museum? Write a novel that will be considered a classic of literature and taught in every school across the nation? Come up with a mathematical theory that will cause a huge advancement in our understanding of the world? Find a cure for disease? Invent something that will improve our lives?

Autistic people have done these things that so-called "normal" people can't do. Who are you to say that somebody is disabled because they have some trouble making friends or can't eye contact? I know lots of people who can't do stuff, but they are not disabled. I know people who can't sing. I know somebody that can't cook or bake. I know people who are bad at math and science. And I admit I can't swim. But to be fair, I can drown better than anybody else.

Seriously, I know I can't swim, so I don't go in the water. The people I know that can't sing have never sung on a stage. The people I know that can't cook or bake always buy something at the grocery store and bring it to the pot luck. You do what you're good at and avoid the things you suck at. Just because you are bad at something it doesn't mean you are disabled. It just means you need help with it.

This essay is being written to give hope and not to give people excuses. I don't want to hear about how I am not as severely autistic as your kid. I don't want to hear how your kid can't do something. Of course, your kid can't do something. You have already told yourself and your kid that they can't. It has already been decided by you before you and your child have tried.

One of the main points of this essay is to rethink things. In *Star Wars: The Empire Strikes Back*, Luke is on Dagobah as he is being trained by Yoda. Luke's X-Wing sinks deeper into the water. Yoda tells him to use the Force and raise it up out of the water. Luke tells him it is one thing to move rocks with the force. It is another to move a space ship. Yoda responds, "No! No different! Only different in your mind. You must unlearn what you have learned."

We are working with misconceptions and wrong perceptions when it comes to autistic people. I think they can achieve great things. They have in the past. The only difference was that we didn't put a label on people and set our expectations low for them. Autism can do amazing things. We just have to believe it can and release the power of autism to do what it is supposed to do.

Difference vs. Disability

Since I was born in 1978, I grew up not being diagnosed with autism. My parents knew I was a little different, but my differences were somehow inherited. My mother knew I had qualities that were similar to her older brother, but he had never been diagnosed with anything. And my mother didn't want to get me diagnosed either out of a fear of me being medicated or because I seemed to get better. My grandparents could recognize that I had qualities similar to my great-grandfather, but they would just assume I had inherited some quirks instead of a form of autism.

I wouldn't actually be diagnosed until I was thirty-four years old. As soon as I found out there was a label for it, some people asked me what that would mean for me. I told them it wouldn't change anything. And it shouldn't change anything. I had Asperger's Syndrome, which is now just part of the Autism Spectrum.

I'm writing this essay to discuss my own struggles, but to also discuss my own successes. You see, autism isn't new. We have begun to think about it differently, but I'm not sure we have started to think about it correctly. I expect this essay to encourage some people, but I know it will also anger some parents. I'm going to be writing this essay from the perspective as somebody on the spectrum instead of as a neurotypical person (a non-autistic person).

I will also be writing this essay as somebody that would be considered high-functioning by these neurotypical people. Some people might say that I can't truly understand autism because I am not severely autistic or low-functioning. I don't believe in the high-functioning and low-functioning labels. It is placing labels on people and what we think somebody is capable of. This limits the perceived low-functioning person and doesn't allow them to reach their full potential. I would rather see somebody succeed instead of fall victim to a non-existent label.

I also might anger some people in that I don't consider autism a disease or a disability. Again, these are limiting the full potential of the individual that you are claiming you are trying to help. I admit autistic people need some special help, but every person needs help at various points in their life. And I will explain my reasoning behind these points.

History

If you read anything online, it will most likely tell you that autism is reaching epidemic proportions. Currently, 1 in 88 people will be diagnosed as having an Autism Spectrum Disorder. There is a 5 to 1 ratio within this 1 in 88 that men will be more affected than women.

Now, there are several ways we could look at these statistics. We could look at it from the alarmist point of view and see autism is on a very rapid rise. The possibility of you having a child with autism is very likely. We've got to find a reason for this. It could be the environment or child vaccines. Something is going on, though, that is causing all of these autistic children to be born.

I don't exactly buy into the alarmist/epidemic theory. In the first place, autism has existed throughout history. Some of the famous people believed to be on the Autism Spectrum include Albert Einstein, Thomas Jefferson, Isaac Newton, Mark Twain, Henry Ford, Thomas Edison, Michelangelo, Jane Austen, Mozart, Hans Christian Andersen, and others. Historians are basing this on the behavior of these famous people.

It is logical that if famous people (who we can study because they were considered important enough from a historical point of view to have been studied in terms of a biography), then non-famous everyday people would also have had some sort of autism throughout history. I can trace my autism back to at least my great-grandfather on my mother's side.

If autism has existed throughout history before pollution and vaccines, then there has to be a more hereditary quality to it than something else we are doing. Also, we have become more aware of autism as a society, so we are now getting our children tested for it. This is going to make more people receive a diagnosis than there would have been before. Is autism actually becoming more of an epidemic, or are we diagnosing it more? I mean, I went undiagnosed for over thirty years. The same is true for Dan Aykroyd and Susan Boyle. I got tested because I heard some discussion of Asperger's Syndrome and began to think that maybe my quirks weren't just family oddities or artistic tendencies. What if I am partly the way I am because of an actual medical term?

One of the main points I will be making in this essay is rethinking the way we are looking at something. The way we see something impacts how we think about it. Some people used to think the world was flat. Then some others thought that it could be round. Even though the world is round, it took some time for the people who saw the world as being flat to realize that it was actually round. They were stuck in a false perception.

You might think you are a normal, neurotypical person, which would make you better than me, a person with autism. But what if my autism allows me to see the world is round faster than you because you can't shake the perception that you have about the world?

Disease and Disability

Dictionary.com defines "disease" as "a disordered or incorrectly functioning organ, part, structure, or system of the body resulting from the effect of genetic or developmental errors, infection, poisons, nutritional deficiency or imbalance, toxicity, or unfavorable environmental factors; illness; sickness; ailment."

Now let's look at autism from this definition. Autism seems to impact the brain. If we look at the first part of the definition, then autism would be a disease if the autistic brain were a disordered or incorrectly functioning brain. There seems to be no evidence for this. Examples of this would include the brains of Albert Einstein and other autistic people. Even my own brain, though it has autism, was able to outperform the majority of students I was in class with. I was primarily a straight A student, except for a B in Geometry. I graduated college with a 3.89 GPA. I also did all of this with very little studying.

There doesn't seem to be a problem with the brain not functioning in autistic people. Even if we look at the autistic brain being different because of genetic or developmental errors, it is still hard to make the case for autism being a disease. Einstein had delayed speech in the same way other people on the spectrum have had delayed speech. The difference is that we are looking at development issues from the perspective of a social construct. We are comparing our children to the children of our friends. We don't allow children to grow at their own pace. We have books and websites telling us where children should be. Before that, children were allowed to grow at their own pace.

I'm not saying you shouldn't get speech therapy and other developmental help for children who are not reaching developmental milestones by certain times. But we cannot write off somebody just because they don't develop at the same pace as somebody else. It's the difference between somebody needs some help versus writing them off as disabled for life. Some people who have been developmentally delayed have gone on to do great things. Our goal should be to get the delayed people to the point where they can succeed.

If we look at the rest of the definition of "disease" in terms of the autistic brain, we can't really say that the autistic mind is full of "infection, poisons, nutritional deficiency or imbalance, toxicity, or unfavorable environmental factors; illness; sickness; ailment." There is nothing about autism that decreases the length of life or the quality of life of the individual. It's not like Alzheimer's, liver disease, kidney disease, or anything else that would shorten a person's life. You can't treat autism in the same way you would a virus or a cancer.

Those neurotypical people out there, who are stuck in your perception of autism, might argue that autism does decrease the quality of life of those impacted because it's a disability. Again, prove to me it is a disability. Look at the definition of autism according to Dictionary.com. "Psychiatry- a pervasive developmental disorder of children, characterized by impaired communication, excessive rigidity, and emotional detachment: now considered one of the autism spectrum disorders. Or a tendency to view life in terms of one's own needs and desires."

Where is the disability? Autism is a social and communication difference. Oh no! Somebody doesn't make friends as easily as somebody else. Somebody doesn't see the need for making chit-chat. Oh no! If somebody says, "drag racing", my mind immediately thinks of guys in dresses and high heels running a race. I process all of the various meanings of a word as somebody is talking to me. There is a sign at the mall that reads, "Watch batteries repaired." I interpret the sign initially as I could watch batteries being repaired. I then have to realize that "watch" is a noun and not a verb. I could get the battery of my watch repaired.

If we look at the second definition of autism as "a tendency to view life in terms of one's own needs and desires", we again see that there isn't a disability. Somebody perceives the world from the view of an individual instead of society. It's psychology versus sociology. Is society more important than the individual?

This is not saying that autistic people do not have issues in society and need help. But autism isn't like being deaf, blind, or being in a wheelchair. It is a learning difference and a difference in perception, but we wouldn't consider a blind person an idiot if we presented visual information to them and then tested them on it. We would recognize the blind person can't learn like that and change the way we teach them. We logically need to do the same thing with autism.

I will talk more about autistic behavior and autistic limitations later, but I feel it is more important to talk about education first.

The Education System

I'm not an educator, and I have never had any desire to be a teacher. I never had any problems in school, except for Geometry. It was never logical to me, plus I never saw a real world use for it except in the construction or manufacturing fields, which I never had any desire to go into. Learning was easy for me, and I was never really challenged in school.

I have heard there are other autistic children like this. Recently there was an autistic student placed in special education classes because he was different. It wasn't that he wasn't smart. If anything, he was too smart and getting bored waiting for the other students to catch up to him. His mother advocated for him, though. He ended up getting out of the special education classes, completing all of the high school math courses in two weeks, and entered college when he was fourteen.

I don't think the education system knows what to do with autistic people. This is partly because there has been more of a focus on group projects and other social activities in school than in actual learning. I'm sorry, but I never learned anything when I worked on a group project. You have to struggle to find a time to meet with the other people. Somebody always shows up late or never shows.

And I have never really learned anything about the subject, except for the one part I worked on. Group projects become a division of labor instead of any sort of actually working together. This is not going to benefit an autistic person in terms of learning.

And if you have an emphasis on class participation, this is not really going to help the autistic person. You will be grading somebody in an area where they have issues without actually grading them on what they know.

I'm not saying this to say that working together as a team or participating in a discussion are not important. It is. These are skills that the autistic person should acquire. But our society has changed to where these are more important than the actual learning process. We are concerned about social things instead of actual education. An autistic person is not going to prosper in a situation like this.

Look at today's children's programming. Most of Nick Jr.'s programming starts with a blurb saying the show teaches social and emotional skills. We are focusing on people fitting in instead of learning letters, numbers, shapes, and other factual things.

If you want to know why bullying seems to have increased in today's society, you only have to look at what we are teaching our children about social skills and belonging. We have lost the sense of somebody being different and unique. This is going to make the people that are different stand out more.

Bullying is not happening in isolation. A girl can be gang raped at a party. The event is a spectator sport with it even being videotaped, but yet nobody says anything while it is happening. It would defy society. We can't rock the societal boat, even if something is morally and legally wrong.

There was a case in England of a young man with Asperger's. It was his 18th birthday. Some of the people at the party doused him in oils, wrote gay slurs on him, and then lit him on fire. He later died. This didn't happen in some darkened corner of the party or in a room secluded from other people. It happened out in the open for all of the guests to see. Nobody did anything to stop it.

When I was growing up, I was different. The difference was that society was more willing to accept people that were different. Then again, I grew up in a time before school shootings and we feared what is different. Instead, when I was being bullied, I had the girls in my class coming to my defense and shaming the guys who were bigger than I was into leaving me alone. I was different, but I was likable and never feared.

I do think we need a change in the culture of education. Bullying isn't going to stop. We are teaching children they need to conform instead of to think for themselves and to question things. We are turning children into parrots instead of fostering creative thinking in them.

It might be because I never had trouble learning, but I don't really believe in learning disabilities like ADD or ADHD. I have had friends who have been diagnosed with this. They have the ability to memorize things they want to learn. They just struggle memorizing things they don't want to learn. This seems to indicate they can memorize and repeat facts, when they want to. The diagnosis becomes a crutch to where they get a free pass for things they don't want to do.

It might be because I'm autistic, but I'm not going to apologize for saying that. It is simple logic. You can't tell me you have ADD or ADHD and can't learn because you can't focus and then tell me random football facts or quote complete movies when you have clearly spent a great deal of your time and effort learning these things.

Here's a newsflash for parents and teachers. Most students don't want to be in school. They would rather be doing other things they enjoy more. One of the reasons I

14

enjoyed school was that I was grew up in a house that valued education. I was taught that education would help me later in life. With an education, I could go and do whatever I wanted to do in life. If I got in trouble in school, I got in trouble at home. This has changed in our society. If a kid gets in trouble, we are now yelling at the teacher. Children are running the education system.

Like autism, I don't think something like ADD or ADHD is going to suddenly spring up in our species. It would have to have been around for a while. Why has it suddenly become an issue? Have we changed how we are teaching? Are we starting children to school too early to keep from paying day care expenses? Are we letting TV, movies, iPads, and any other whim the child wants to be entertained with dictate what happens in the household?

I'm sorry, but when I was a kid, we didn't have all day children's programming, computers, DVDs or blu-rays, video games, and iPads. I understood I couldn't always do what I wanted to do. I was taught there were times I had to be quiet and not do the things I wanted to do. That was part of being in society.

In the upcoming chapters, I will be discussing sensory issues, behavior issues, and some current theories on the autistic brain. I have not seen anything in my own experiences or in reading to suggest autism means lesser intelligence. We need to stop thinking about it in those terms.

Autistic people will learn differently, and different autistic people will learn in different ways. We can't have a one size fits all educational plan when it comes to autism. It impacts everybody differently.

I also think autism will have a varying degree of intelligence among the population in the same way there would be varying intelligence among neurotypical people. This has nothing to do with high-functioning and low-functioning labels. Those labels are based on perceptions of how well somebody interacts in society, and a lot of times they have to do with how much somebody communicates, which again doesn't reflect actual intelligence. I will discuss this more in the next chapter. What I want to point out is that there will be a range of IQs among people on the spectrum despite where a doctor might place them on the spectrum. There will be your A students, your B and C students, and the D and F students.

In order to help autistic students, as well as neurotypical students, we are going to have to actually look at how people learn and make sure they are in the proper classes. The one size fits all classroom isn't going to be cutting it anymore. With genius levels of intelligence being found among some segments of the autism community, we need to start thinking about challenging the autistic student instead of writing them off. We cannot associate autism with stupidity.

Frankly, if I am not intellectually stimulated, I tend to slip into my own thoughts. Boredom is one of the worst things you can have happen to an autistic person. I will discuss this more in the section about autistic behavior. I just want to bring up the possibility that maybe we are limiting autistic people by not understanding them correctly.

We have a tendency to look at autism from the point of view of the neurotypical person instead of from the point of view of the autistic person. What if we can change our view and learn something new about autism that could radically change our world?

In terms of education, I would encourage various forms of artistic expression for autistic people. For one thing, art allows the opportunity to get into the mind of the autistic person. They will express themselves and create things that give you an insight into their thinking.

Art is also a collaborative thing, especially in the musical arts. You play alongside other people and learn the value of working together. But instead of it being a group project, the autistic person can do something they love and not have the pressure of being verbal or communicating with somebody else.

Artists also tend to be more accepting of people who are different or a little quirky. With a common interest like drawing, painting, music, or other arts, the autistic person can learn social skills by talking about something they like with another person.

If we are ever going to truly help autistic students, we need to stop trying to make them neurotypical. We need to embrace the autism and see what we can learn about the person. We need to release the power of the individual.

Throughout history autism has existed. Yes, there will be limitations and struggles with autistic people, but there is also strength. We need to harness the strength and release the superhero that is within the autistic individual. I admit those autistic behaviors people often complain about are the Kryptonite of the autistic people, but I also believe there is a Superman within each of us that is on the spectrum. We just need the proper guidance to get there. And I will explain this more later.

The Importance of Difference

The reason I would prefer for autism to be considered a difference is because that is how all of the literature I have read and the doctors I have talked to have explained it. Basically the autistic brain is wired differently. They do not know yet why it is. They do know there is a difference in the brain chemistry. Medication intended for one thing in neurotypical people seems to do something entirely different in autistic people.

I understand the frustration of neurotypical people with the behavior of autistic people, but you must understand that autistic people can achieve great things. Autism isn't something to be feared, cured, or wiped out.

Think about it from my point of view. Would you want to cure your child of being different if the being different were something like homosexuality? As a society, we would be disturbed by that thought. But we don't seem to have that mentality when it comes to autism. Instead we talk about it being a disability and a disease.

I admit I have limitations and struggles. But I hate to point out the obvious that everybody in life has limitations and struggles. That is the nature of life. All we can decide to do with the circumstances we have been given is to do the best that we can and have some sort of faith there is a reason for us being the way we are. I was born with higher intelligence than most people, but this is offset by less social skills. Still through it all, I am well liked and can still get along with people.

I could pass for being neurotypical. It's just that I don't see the reason to deny my autistic qualities. For the most part, I have been able to keep my meltdowns in private. I can mask my sensory issues. In fact, when I tell most people I am autistic, they don't believe me. They have some preconceived notion of what an autistic person should be.

I'm not willing to let others like me be stereotyped. I would rather define what autism can do and dispel the general preconceptions and prejudices.

Focus Becomes Reality

In *Star Wars Episode 1: The Phantom Menace*, Qui-Gon tells Jar Jar Binks, "The ability to speak does not make you intelligent." This is a very true statement. And the opposite is also true. "The ability to not speak does not make you unintelligent."

Autism is being looked at as a spectrum with high functioning and low functioning. This is a concept developed by non-autistic people to define autistic people in some attempt to have labels on them. The inability to speak would put you more on the low functioning end of the spectrum. There are examples of extremely brilliant autistic people who do not speak. They can communicate through a keyboard perfectly fine. They type what they want to say, and a computer system reproduces the words for other people to hear. They, therefore, understand language, grammar, spelling, and sentence structure. They are not idiots.

This seems to indicate that they have a normal intelligence based on how they can comprehend language and use it properly, even if they do not speak. They can spell and use language properly to form sentences, which shows signs of greater intelligence than most of the people who text today. But, yet, we are predisposed to think that somebody who doesn't speak is unintelligent. The old saying is deaf and dumb.

Now, let's look at this problem from the perspective of the autistic person. At the heart of autism is a problem with social skills, difficulty communicating, and sensory issues. Speaking is an odd thing. It creates sound inside your head. Think about the sensory issues related to this. If an autistic person has problems with loud noises outside of their body, can you imagine what it must be like for their vocal chords to be producing sounds inside of their own body?

19

There are times I think I am talking at an acceptable audible level. Others tell me that I am too quiet. If I talk louder, sometimes I give off the impression of being angry, even if I'm not angry. It's just that I don't know how to increase volume without talking with more force. Plus, talking louder causes me to spend more of my energy producing the louder sounds. It's not that I just have to talk to somebody else, I now have to concentrate to make sure I am at the proper sound level. All of this makes my speech seem more unnatural, which gives off the impression of me being angry.

This is the case, unless I am inside of a mask. Apparently, when I put on my Batman costume, I talk louder to where I am almost shouting at people. I didn't really know this. With my ears muffled, I was producing the same sound levels I usually heard. It's like I have naturally found that appropriate volume of taking based on the years of people telling me to speak up.

What I am trying to point out is the possibility that talking might fall under the sensory issues of an autistic person. Maybe we need to stop thinking about language as only a developmental issue. Maybe there is a sensory issue to it as well. A baby will cry before it learns how to speak. Maybe some research should be done to see if children are actually delayed in speech or choosing not to speak because the act of creating sound with your vocal chords is unpleasant to the person. As it is right now, we are looking at the problem of delayed speech as a non-autistic person sees it and understands human development. We are not looking at it from the perspective of the autistic person. Regardless of why the person isn't speaking, I still recommend speech therapy.

Recent research has also started to focus on musical therapy for non-verbal autistic children. Basically the reproduction of sound through music is being taught instead of teaching language directly. Why? What is the difference? Singing expresses emotions through the use of words, but it does so without exactly communicating with somebody else. It is taking the social function away from language until the person gets used to using language. Also musical language is more pleasing to the ear than random spoken words.

I can tell you this from my own childhood. I would zone out when I was a child. I would rock back and forth while listening to records over and over again. I wouldn't even respond to my own name. I recently asked my mom what songs I was listening to. She said it would be things that would be considered oldies now like the Beatles, Elton John, etc.

As a writer, I will tell you that my use of language has been influenced by musicians. I hear rhythms and tones when people speak. It is a form of music. Language is also lyrical and flows, even as it is simply being spoken. And if you look at my punctuation, you will notice that I use commas and periods as a sort of musical rest. That is how I hear words and sentences. I also arrange my phrases to break up the sentences into a more lyrical form.

Also, when I was a child, I used to wear foot braces. We had wood paneling on the walls at the time. I went to sleep by humming and kicking my braces against the wall. I was too young to remember this, but I seemed to be naturally doing something with music to calm myself and to get myself to sleep.

I was able to speak as a child. I wasn't delayed, but I still somehow used music as a child as a way to understand the world around me or to escape from the world around me.

If we look at language in people on the autism spectrum, we see a wide array of language use and understanding. The so-called higher functioning autistics, like those who used to be labeled as having Asperger's Syndrome, were noted for an advanced use of language.

They would use bigger and more mature words than other children their own age. The lower functioning autistics would be defined by their lack of use of language.

Now, let's work from a radical theory. If we get rid of the terms "low-functioning" and "high-functioning" and just look at variations in speech and reproduced sounds from autistics, what can we discover about speech and autism? There will naturally be a difference in intelligence across the spectrum. There is a difference in intelligence throughout people in society. We, however, do not declare somebody of a lower and yet acceptable level of intelligence to be disabled when they are compared to somebody else of higher IQ. Let's say it is somebody with an IQ of 90 and an IQ of 125. Instead, we would group them with the higher intelligence people, if we were conducting research. Let's do the same with autism and see what we can learn.

Let's work off of the theory that autism is autism. Although a so-called higher functioning autistic is thought to be better capable of making it in society and not as severely disabled as the low functioning autistic, what if the higher functioning is able to help us to better understand the lower functioning? If you have somebody on the spectrum who is better able to communicate than somebody that isn't, then why can't you use their ability to communicate as a way to better understand the person who isn't communicating?

This is really why I would like to get rid of the low functioning and high functioning terms. My mom doesn't like that I call myself autistic. She has seen other people who would be considered more severely autistic. They have real problems. I'm just a little different. But what if I'm not really that different from the more severely autistic person? What if my differences and quirks that non-autistic people notice and my similarities with autistic people could be used as a bridge between the severely autistic and the normal people? What if I am just better at understanding the world around me and expressing my feelings, frustrations, sensations, and experiences?

We know there is something going on with speech with people on the spectrum. Some don't talk. Some talk a lot, even when others aren't listening. Some have advanced language usage. Some talk in voices that aren't their own. They mimic characters they have seen in TV and movies. They are actually pretending to be somebody else. There is something going on with speech and autism. We're just too focused on the various aspects of autism and placing people on a segment of a spectrum to fully understand how these differences in speech might actually point to a commonality. What is happening in the autistic mind when it comes to speech?

I want to stop here for a minute and bring up something else that Qui-Gon said. "Your focus becomes your reality." One of the things I want parents to understand is that changing how you look at autism can change how you perceive your child and their behavior. This is one of the reasons why I want to get rid of "disability" and "disease" when we talk about autism. These words cause children to be seen a certain way, and how we see something impacts the way we act towards it. If we think of the autistic child as disabled and never able to achieve much in life, that child will never be able to reach their full potential and accomplish things in life. We have already predetermined them to fail. What we focus on becomes our reality.

I understand it is frustrating that your child isn't talking and he's the same age as your best friend's kid, who is speaking. I know you want your child to talk to you and use his own voice instead of imitating a cartoon character and pretending to be somebody else as they are interacting with you. But you are going to have to meet the autistic person at least half way, if not more than half way, in order to build a successful relationship with your own child.

And there is another reason that I don't like for autism to be defined as a disability or a disease. There is parental guilt where the parents feel somehow responsible for their children being different. Disease implies a cause for the symptoms and a possible cure. Autism has existed throughout history, even if it wasn't defined as autism. It existed before vaccines and air pollution. Parents need to absolve themselves from this guilt. Hating yourself for the way your child is does not help your child. Loving your child for the way they are does help them. Remember your focus determines your reality.

Now looking at some of the issues that frustrate parents about their autistic children, let's see if we can't find productive ways to better understand the child and to communicate with them better. Again, I am going to be working off of the theory that autism is autism. Let's ignore the labels of high functioning and low functioning. And let's work off of the theory that, although autism exhibits itself differently in every person with autism, there will be common threads among autism in general. There is a saying that goes, "If you have met one person with autism, you have met one person with autism." The quirks and sensitivities in autism will vary from person to person. But there also has to be something common among autistic people to make them autistic.

Looking again at speech, we can theorize various reasons why somebody with autism might not speak. Many things go into speaking. Part of it is auditory. Depending on how autism impacts the person, they may not like the way their voice sounds in their head and decide not to talk. If you have a person sensitive to sound, which is common with autism, it might be disturbing to them to have sound reproduced inside of their own head. This is not farfetched. The sounds that bother me the most are not necessarily loud noises. I get bothered by vibrating noises like loud bass noises or the sound of the wheels hitting the road. This is essentially what your voice is going to be doing as your vocal chords are going to be vibrating within your head.

There is also a social function to speaking. If one of the symptoms of autism is impaired social interaction, then it only makes sense that speaking might be delayed or that the person might find new ways of speaking and interacting, like impersonating other people or characters.

As a child, I would do character voices. I did the Woody Woodpecker laugh. I talked like Pee Wee Herman. I did the Emmanuel Lewis laugh from *Webster.* I also played with puppets and ventriloquist dolls.

There might be some benefit to autistics by playing with puppets or interacting with puppets. One of the famous people that makes the list of suspected of having autism is Jim Henson. As a child, I loved the Muppets. They were my first obsession. I used to get up at 5:30 in the morning on Sundays and change the antenna so that I could watch *The Muppet Show*. After it was over, I would change the antenna back and go to bed. My parents were fully aware of this.

Looking back on my own life, I can see how I would play with puppets or ventriloquist dolls. When I was about eight, my grandmother taught me how to sew. I then started to make my own sock puppets from the socks of my family members that had gotten holes in them. I would then use scraps of material that my grandmother no longer needed. I didn't put on puppet shows with the characters I created. I interacted with other people with the puppets, or talked to the puppet and interacted with it.

I can watch old home movies of my uncle, who is probably autistic even though he hasn't been tested, and see that he too had an interest in puppetry and ventriloquist dolls. I didn't spend that much time with my uncle as a child. I couldn't have picked up the behavior from him.

What if the puppet or ventriloquist doll allows the autistic person to communicate with other people without the social pressure of the autistic person actually communicating with the other person? What if puppetry could actually help the more non-verbal autistic people to become more verbal?

One of the things that people learned from *Sesame Street* is that children see the puppet attached to the person, but they only look at the puppet and not the performer. Several years ago, I bought a full body puppet of Grover from *Sesame Street*. My youngest nephew has always been a little bit behind other children. He hasn't been diagnosed with any autism spectrum disorder, but he has many of the same characteristics that I have exhibited over the years.

When he was younger, I would take over my Grover puppet and perform it for him. I even did the Grover voice. Even though I am his uncle, I stopped existing as soon as I had the puppet on my hand. He would interact with the puppet in ways that he would never do with me. He would ask Grover questions and would talk to him as if he was his best friend. The other amazing thing I discovered was that my nephew would voluntarily hug Grover, even though he would never run up to other family members and hug them. You could hug my nephew and get a hug if you asked for one, but the act of hugging was never initiated on his part on his own.

Today's children's programming has a focus on social and emotional skills. If you have an autistic child, you might want to consider showing them older episodes of *Sesame Street*. These shows can be found on DVDs and some streaming services. They will carry the warning that the shows will not meet the educational needs of today's children. What you might be doing, though, is helping to teach your child letters, numbers, rhyming, shapes, and other things in a way that an autistic person could learn better.

Sometimes autistics respond better to other autistic people. Use the older Jim Henson episodes to help today's autistic children to at least learn some of the basics they will need to know before entering school. The social and emotional skills can be taught later, especially when the autistic person is having the most difficulty in these areas. Get the child used to learning or to become familiar with the information before worrying about how they are interacting with other people.

And if you have an autistic child, see if interacting with puppets helps them interact with other people. And instead of worrying about how your child might be interacting with objects instead of people, concentrate on what your child is saying to the object that is being performed by a human. It will give you an insight into what the person is thinking, especially when they don't seem to be communicating in any other way.

There's a documentary about a boy with autism that talks to lampposts. When I was younger, I shared a bedroom with my brother. When I couldn't sleep, I would talk to him. Then he got upset with me for talking to him. So I started talking to the moon. I knew perfectly well that I was really talking to my brother and not the moon, but transferring who I was talking to still allowed me to say the things I was thinking about. What if we rethink autism and see if allowing autistic people to talk to inanimate objects helps them to become more verbal? But to get this to work, the non-autistic people are going to have to focus on what the child is saying and not on what they are saying it to.

In addition to puppetry, I would suggest using music to teach language, emotions, and social interactions. There have been musicians throughout history who have exhibited autistic traits. Mozart and Beethoven would be classical examples of this. Bob Dylan is a more modern example of somebody with autistic qualities. These people haven't been tested for autism because they were born

27

before autism became a diagnosis. People who would diagnose autism just look at their biographies and behavior. So what if musical therapy could help somebody who wasn't communicating to start talking about what they are feeling?

Everybody likes music. There are times in our lives where we can't express what we are feeling or going through, and yet we can usually find a song that fits our situation exactly. Since autistic people are humans, their response is going to be the same to music. They may not be able to verbalize it, but if we can teach them music and to sing about their inner struggles, maybe we can better understand them and what they are going through in life.

When I was a child, I guess my mother thought I was different. I wasn't socializing the way I should be. She then decided to give me piano lessons. I think she thought I was extremely shy. Learning how to play the piano might help to make me feel more confident or something. I'm not exactly sure what her thinking was, but I got the hint from the way she told me the story when I was older that there was at least some form of musical therapy to get me out of my shell. I just remember taking piano lessons around the time I started kindergarten and not knowing why I was taking them exactly.

What I remember of my childhood was an emphasis in allowing me to explore the arts. I was encouraged to write, draw, color, play music, or enjoy the arts in any mode available. Solitary and quiet activities were not frowned upon. Today there is an emphasis on children and social skills, which has its merits, but there is also a need for autistic people to have this quiet time to pursue their own interests. Sometimes my mom doesn't agree with my artistic projects, but I do need them to keep my own sanity and to work out emotions and problems I face in life. Sometimes I need to solve my own problems by working through them in solitude instead of talking about them to somebody else. It's a difference in communicating and understanding myself.

There are things we can do to help autistic children with social and emotional skills. We just might have to go about it in a different way, instead of looking at the same problem in the same way we always have. The focus before has been on making the autistic person "normal" by thinking their brains work the same way a non-autistic person's works. Research is starting to show that autism is a difference in understanding and perceiving the world. We need to meet the problem from the perspective of the autistic person and not from the perspective of the non-autistic person who is trying to cure them.

And maybe one of the biggest things we need to do is to stop thinking that because somebody doesn't speak that it means they are unintelligent or of a lessor intelligence. Talking is a social skill that has nothing to do with intelligence. A characteristic of autism is social impairment. We can't write off the autistic person who doesn't talk as being stupid and unable to achieve great things in life. Even Albert Einstein, who is believed to also be autistic, didn't speak until he was three or four.

I want to add the caveat here that there will be severely autistic people and even mildly autistic people who will need help. I have never advocated that they don't need help making it in the world. I am just not willing to believe that something that is a spectrum like autism, which can produce great scientists, mathematicians, musicians, and artists, can be only considered a disease or a disability. There are benefits to autism. We just need to change society and how it views autism to help the autistic individual, which will end up helping society.

I don't want to see people written off because they do not conform to what we think a person should be. Let's try to get inside of their world and see what we can learn about them.

I know there is a concern about autistic people getting jobs. If somebody is great at science, encourage that. If they are great at singing, encourage that. There are ways to make money with the natural talents people have. We have to stop focusing on the negative and the actual grades somebody gets. Both Einstein and Stephen Hawking got bad grades in school, and yet we consider them geniuses. We cannot judge people entirely by academic success. There are people who will not fit the mold and need the freedom to become great at whatever it is that they were born to do.

Those Autistic Behaviors

How do you begin to explain what it is like to be autistic to somebody that is normal? I think the best I can do is to tell them to watch *Man of Steel*. When a young Clark Kent sees and hears everything to where he has a meltdown, you will somewhat know what it is like to have sensory issues.

In large groups of people where everybody is talking, I have a hard time filtering out the conversations. I hear what the people I am talking to are saying, but I also hear the people around us talking at the same sort of level. I hear the background music, the sound of traffic, the sound of forks hitting china, ice hitting the side of the glass, and a multitude of other sounds all at once.

Even in quiet settings like at home, I can be upstairs in my parents' house and hear them talking downstairs. They aren't yelling at each other. They are talking at a normal level of conversation, but I can hear them the same as if I were in the room with them. Last week my mom thought I was in the living room while she was in the kitchen. I was upstairs, but I heard everything she said. When she realized I wasn't in the next room, she stopped talking and waited for me to come back down. When I came downstairs, I repeated everything she had said and thought I hadn't heard. I then picked up the conversation from where she had started it five minutes before, even though she thought I had never heard her due to the distance between our locations.

Bright lights bother me. Bright sunny days bother me. It's not that I don't enjoy the sunshine. It's just brighter than what I would like and creates glare on things. If somebody says hi to me as they are passing in a car, I will probably have a hard time noticing who it is. The brightness of the sun does that to me.

The common theory of autistic people not sensing the world is starting to change to where it is believed that autistic people are sensing the world too much. There is also the theory that maybe autistic don't lack empathy, but that we feel too much. Autistics are then stuck in a world where senses are heightened and we have to try to act like we are normal. If we sometimes miss out on appropriate behavior, it could be due to the fact we are trying to control our senses as we are being barraged by the world around us.

I don't want to excuse autistic meltdowns. I only want to help the non-autistic people to understand some of the behavior.

One of the things I see parents complain about with their autistic children is their eating habits. Eating is a sensory issue. There are foods I don't necessarily dislike because of their taste. I don't like the way it chews. Cooked carrots are okay, but I don't like them raw. It's the texture. White creamy substances coming towards my mouth freaks me out. I don't like Ranch dressing, mayo, or sour cream. Now, if you mix it up in something, I'm okay with it. Tuna salad is fine, and so are potatoes with the sour cream mixed throughout. I even like the taste of Ranch, if it is not in liquid form. Give me a chicken coated with a dry, Ranch seasoning, and I will eat it.

Other autistic people will eat hamburgers, but they won't eat meat loaf. In their mind, these two things are completely different things. They like one, but they aren't willing to try the other because it is different. My nephew won't eat cold things. He usually leaves his milk out for a little bit to where it is not too cold. Applesauce is okay, but actual apples are not.

What I can tell you about being autistic and eating is that there is a logic to what I am willing to try and not try. It is an internal logic and not based on an actual logic. Fighting with your child about food is going to be frustrating.

If you get me upset before a meal time, I just won't eat. Sometimes I get bored with food. It's not that I'm not hungry. I will eat enough to curb the hunger, but the actual act of eating and enjoying food just isn't there. There's no new thrill to eating. I've been there and done that to where I just can't get excited about eating.

Other times, I am too preoccupied with other things to worry about eating. My focus is on thinking, solving a problem, or working on a project. I won't notice that I am hungry. One of the problems with autism is that you can be extremely sensitive to some things and not sensitive to others. Loud noises and bright lights might cause me more pain than actual physical pain or discomfort like being hungry. Hypersensitivity (over sensitive) and hyposensitivity (under sensitive) will affect each autistic person differently.

What most parents don't understand about hypersensitivity is that once the child becomes stimulated by the world around them, it is often hard for them to quiet down afterwards. There is a reason that a lot of autistic people have a hard time sleeping. It's not uncommon for it to take two hours or more for me to fall asleep. When I was a child, I would talk to my brother to pass the time. When he got angry at me, I talked to the moon. I knew I couldn't really talk to the moon, but if I said I was talking to the moon, then my brother couldn't yell at me for really talking to him. My talk was directed to the moon and not to him.

Eventually he would fall asleep, and I would just lay in bed waiting to fall asleep. Then I would hear *Leave It to Beaver* come on in the living room. I would sneak down the hall and watch it undetected from my parents. Sometimes they would let me watch it with them before sending me back to bed. It didn't seem to matter that this was two hours after having actually put me to bed.

I read an article today that researchers are thinking autistic people have a hard time getting their minds to settle down. There's introspection and reflecting on the events of the day that keeps their minds racing. There is also the theory that they have been overstimulated by sensory issues that it takes longer for the autistic brain to settle down. It's not that the child is trying to be disobedient by not going to sleep. Sleep is just not an easy thing for autistic people to do, even when we are really tired. I can nap easier than I can actually go to bed at night.

And then there are those other behaviors, which I don't really know how to explain. It involves the meltdowns and the emotional bursts that sometimes have nothing to do with what the person is really upset about.

There are theories into why autistic people have meltdowns. I don't know which one is correct. One of the more recent ones has to do with this intense world theory in which autistic people feel too much, whether it is emotions or sensations.

And how do I even begin to explain what a meltdown feels like so that it can help the non-autistic person to understand?

Some people have described people with Asperger's as being like Spock from *Star Trek*. I have never really watched the old series. I have watched the new movies. I do relate to Spock in those, especially when he loses his temper. It is like he is trying to reconcile the logical Vulcan side of himself with his human emotional side.

We can hold logic as an ideal. I do pride myself on trying to make decisions based on reason and logic instead of emotions. As much as emotions can be a good thing, it can cloud our judgment and blind us to where we do not make the right decision.

Part of my meltdowns probably come from a buildup of emotions that just finally need to be expressed.

They have been repressed for so long, though, that I tend I blow up.

My meltdowns have always reminded me of Anakin Skywalker/Darth Vader. I know there is good in me. As much as I would like to make the world a better place, my emotions get the best of me. I then have the meltdown and do things I regret, whether it is harming myself by hitting myself on the head, punching the wall, throwing things. After the meltdown, I know I have given into my anger. I also recognize the fact that I am considerably stronger when I am angry. I fully recognize the strength and the power I have that comes from being angry. I also understand there is a tendency to pussy foot around autistic people and to not discuss the explosions and meltdowns. It is like they can be excused for their behavior. I would much rather try to teach people how to handle the emotions and to get the person to a good spot instead of excusing the behavior.

To do this, we will need to reach out to the autistic individual and help to understand them. We need to get them to communicate what is bothering them. We cannot leave them to their own devices and hope they will just grow out of the autism. All heroes need mentors and people to guide them. If we live in fear of the autism and the autistic behavior, I am afraid we will be losing the individual to the dark parts of autism and the feeling of not belonging.

The worst part about identifying with Vader is the feeling of being more machine than man. It is as if you have lost part of your humanity that you can't ever seem to reclaim.

There are times I have been needed to help out, whether it is carrying something heavy or breaking it free. I have joked with my parents that they need to make me angry. I need to release the Hulk. It's not really a joke, though. It's what a full blown meltdown is like. Thinking is replaced by emotions. It is in these moments that it is best to just let me experience the emotions and to get them out of my system. You have to let the Hulk calm down before you come near me again. To interrupt the meltdown can only make it worse. You have to let the autistic person return to their thinking self.

I think the problem with autism is that I feel like the Tin Man from *The Wizard of Oz*. I want a heart because I think I am somehow lacking one. I know I have a brain and can think. I can cry and long for love, but I can't seem to use my brain to realize that I actually have a heart.

There are times I feel like the Beast in *Beauty and the Beast*. I want to be human again. I look at those around me, and I just don't feel like they seem to feel. There is something missing or different about me that always makes me different and somehow not human. It is like there is some spell on me that I am waiting for somebody to break that will make me truly human.

And as we are talking about autistic behavior, let's discuss what Sherlock Holmes describes as a black period. I don't know how best to explain this type of boredom in which the things I usually enjoy doing are not enjoyable. It is as if I need a new high or something to challenge me and to keep my mind occupied.

I suffer from this a lot during breaks or vacations. I would almost rather continue working to keep me doing something or to keep me engaged with people. A couple of years ago my parents visited my grandfather. I was left in town for a week by myself. What few friends I had were out of town for the holidays. I wasn't working because of the Christmas break. I got extremely bored. I got bored to the point that I decided Russian roulette would be a good idea.

I don't want you to think this was your typical Russian roulette. I came up with the idea of a giant roulette wheel that I could spin and throw Russian people on. The

Russians will probably hate me for this, but it is what happens when I get bored. I need something to entertain myself with.

Over this last holiday season, I got bored and decided to revise Jane Austen's *Pride and Prejudice*. I updated the language a little bit to make it more modern. My psychiatrist asked me how long the book was. I told him it was over 400 pages. He was kind of surprised I would do something like that. I told him I was bored.

A lot of my writings happen when I am bored. I am looking for something to entertain myself with. But even as an artist, sometimes I can't find the next great idea. I can tell you have a works that I think are masterpieces. Other works I do because I need something to do with myself. It's not that I don't think they are good. It is more of a way of passing the time than anything else.

I don't think this kind of boredom is uncommon across the spectrum. When you are constantly being barraged by the world around you with the various senses, I think it would be common to find yourself desensitized from time to time and needing to feel a new sort of high. This would be the opposite of the meltdown.

There is a story that Mozart got bored one time and started to get on tables and pretend he was a cat. You just need a new experience.

A certain sort of curiosity comes from these boredom times. I once thought about seeing if I could blow up a balloon with helium, tie a long string onto it, and then light the string on fire. My plan was to do this outside and see if I could have a giant ball of fire in the sky as the helium burned. Unfortunately, I discovered that helium wasn't flammable. I wasn't able to conduct the experiment. I still wouldn't mind to do it, if I could find a flammable gas that would float. It would be like releasing a mini-sun into the sky.

I think parents and mental health professionals should look at the boredom theory for some autistic behavior. I have heard of severely autistic people throwing things out of windows. Why did they do this? It might have seemed like a good idea at the time. Maybe they wanted to see what would happen if you dropped things. How would it fall? Do different things fall differently?

And boredom is not the same as depression. Non-autistic people have to understand this. Depression is a sadness and a loss of something. I've been depressed before. I have also been bored. I have been bored to where I didn't enjoy things I usually enjoy. It's not that I was depressed. I was just looking for something new and exciting to keep me stimulated. I have explored my interests. I have known them to their full extent. I need something more to challenge me.

When I first went to get tested for Asperger's, the psychiatrist put me on anxiety/depression medicine. All the medicine did was make me feel like I had a couple of drinks in me all of the time. I had that nice little buzzed feeling. It still took me a while to get the actual diagnosis because the medical profession is more interested in treating things like anxiety and depression. It took me a while to get the doctor to actually recommend me to somebody to get tested. After the diagnosis, I told the doctor I wanted off of the medication. I was basically told I didn't seem as nervous as I was when I first started seeing him, so the medication seemed to be helping.

The doctor was convinced of the anxiety and depression. He wouldn't see my ease of talking to him as having come from becoming accustomed to him. Seeing him was the first time I had gone to a psychiatrist. I didn't know what to expect. It was a new experience for an autistic person. Once I had gotten used to it, I was more comfortable and seemed less anxious. It had nothing to do with the medication. Even the depression medicine didn't really help. I wasn't depressed. I had bouts of boredom.

The boredom theory should also be looked at in terms of education. You have to keep autistic people engaged. I have heard stories about people on the spectrum who were doing well in school and then started to fall behind. They got bored waiting for the rest of the class to catch up to them. As they got bored, the fell deeper inside their own thoughts.

You see, one of the strengths and potential weaknesses of autism is the ability to focus on something that interests the autistic person. It is the opposite of Attention Deficit. It is Attention Surplus. As I have said before, Jim Henson was believed to have been on the spectrum. As a teenager, he wanted to get into television. He saw an ad for puppeteers for a local station. He hadn't worked with puppets before, so he read two books on puppetry and taught himself how to make and perform puppets within a two week period.

Again, there was the autistic boy who was placed in special education classes because he was getting bored. The non-autistic people thought he was delayed. His mother advocated for him. He ended up doing all of the high school math classes in a two week period before going to college at the age of fourteen. He put four years' worth of studying into a two week period.

In addition to boredom, autistic people can become extremely focused on something. I have been tested for obsessive compulsive disorder. I admit to my obsessions and interests. I have rituals and routines I follow. My video collection is categorized. I have my animated movies by studio with the Disney films in chronological order. It then goes into a comedy section in alphabetical order with each artist's work being in chronological order. I then have all other movies in alphabetical order, unless it is a director

I respect. In that case, they have their own section with their works in chronological order.

When I got the job as a manager at work, I organized my shirts. I separated the short sleeves from the long. I then arranged them by color according to the rainbow (ROYGBIV). Since the whites, blacks, and greys did not fit this scheme, I went from white to grey to black.

I don't think autistic people are OCD. Autistic people probably see the world as chaotic and like to put a little bit of order to it. It provides comfort. I don't expect other people to understand that. My video organization system is mine. I can tell you where any film is. It is important to me, so I gave it organization and order. And, yes, it does bother me if somebody looks at a movie from my collection and doesn't put it back in the proper spot.

If somebody has a meltdown, it might have to do with something not being right. The ritual, routine, organization, or whatever isn't the way it should be. This is upsetting to the autistic person, but it is different from being OCD.

Being able to focus on something like an interest or idea has its benefits. But it also has its limitation. You have to understand that autistic people sometimes do not consider the consequences of their actions. Sometimes that part of the equation doesn't factor in to what they are doing. They become so focused on the idea that they lose sight of the people around them like the kid who was dropping things out of the window. To think about what might happen to those below was not a thought.

Part of this might have to do with an impaired sense of danger or the fight or flight tendency some autistic people have. One Halloween I was walking home dressed like Harry Potter. There was a car circling slowly around me. The stopped in a drive way and turned around. They then stopped alongside of me and said, "Trick or Treat."

I responded, "Happy Halloween." When they were circling me, I was becoming slightly scared, but I wasn't willing to run.

Since I had stopped at Subway on my way home, I was carrying a bag with my sandwich in it. The guy in the car then said, "I want your candy."

I replied, "I don't have any candy."

He then got out of the car, walked over to me, and said, "Well, I want what is in your bag. You're either going to give it to me, or I'm going to beat you up and send you to the hospital."

My autistic brain was now weighing my various options. I could go crazy on him, wave my wand, and shout a spell. In his confusion at my craziness, I could then knee him in the crotch and run off. This plan wasn't the best since I was in my Harry Potter robes. There was a risk of tripping.

I thought about fighting, but it would have been two guys and two girls against me. Even if I took out the first guy by surprise, he had backup and I didn't. This plan was scrapped for the simple numbers. Plus I wasn't angry at the moment. I couldn't have released the Hulk and used my anger to beat my enemies. I would have just gotten beaten up.

My other plan was to negotiate with the terrorist. I offered to split half of my sandwich with him, which he agreed to. So I opened it up, tore it in half, and gave it to him. He got in the car and then drove off.

To be fair, I was only partially robbed. And in a way, I did win that one. Being autistic, my sandwich was plain. It was a turkey and cheese on wheat bread. There were no condiments or vegetables. Never try to rob an autistic person for food. You will usually be disappointed.

I don't know what to do in dangerous situations. I don't think a lot of autistic people do. I heard the other day about a five year old that was about to touch a snake. That sense of being afraid just wasn't there.

And I know there are issues with autistic people walking off in the extreme cold or heat without the proper clothing or supplies. What are you going to do with a group of people who become focused on an idea and can think of nothing else besides that? And if you couple this with other autistic behavior like hypersensitivity or hyposensitivity, how do you get the autistic person to understand the danger involved in the behavior? If the child is less sensitive to cold, they can get frost bite before they even realize they are cold.

Somehow we need to recognize the sensory issues of autistic people and understand how it impacts them. Even being considered high functioning, I acknowledge the fact that if I ever become rich and famous, I will need some sort of guardian to accompany me to larger cities for interviews and stuff. Between the new situations and not recognizing when I am in danger, I will need that person to guide me and to help me. I know my limitations.

I suggest the same thing for other autistic people in new situations. They should have a buddy support system of somebody they can trust. Frankly, it would help with bullying if we could get the autistic person a peer mentor to help guide them through situations. I can tell you that as an autistic, even before I was diagnosed, I would get picked on for being different. It didn't matter if I was just walking down the street. I would have guys in a car drive by me. They would roll the window down and yell something at me. When I was startled, they would drive off laughing at me.

Even animals can tell I'm different. There's a dog that is always chained up on my way to my parents' house. He won't bark at other people, but he will always bark at me. One day, he wasn't tied up. He comes at me like he is going to be attacking me. There were other strangers around, but he singled me out. He got within two feet of me and just barked. Not knowing what else to do, I just stood there. Another stranger walked by us, but the dog was only concerned about me. I was the different one. Even animals can tell that. Sometimes animals may be nicer to me because of my difference. Sometimes they are like humans and want to single me out.

One of the things that would help me greatly would be to have somebody who could explain new social situations to me. I want to make sure I follow the proper dress code and societal rules. I get nervous about not wearing the proper clothes to places. I don't want to be overdressed or underdressed. Clothing helps me to at least somewhat blend in as if I actually belonged there. And I do better with definite social rules like what would have existed during Jane Austen's time.

If we ever decide to truly help autistic people in our society, we are going to have to look at the problem differently. We need to stop asking ourselves, "What can we do to make these people normal?" We need to be asking ourselves, "How are autistic people perceiving the world? What can we do differently to help them fit in better?"

And this might be controversial, but I think we need to stop excusing the meltdowns and other negative autistic behavior as if it can't be prevented. It's not that I don't still have my meltdowns or occasional social problems, but I do make an effort. And it is only fair that if we are asking neurotypical people to make an effort to understand autistic people, then the autistic person should make an effort to fit into society.

I've described my meltdowns before as being like Anakin Skywalker/Darth Vader. When I was growing up and exhibited negative behaviors, my mother told me I was acting like my uncle. She thought I would pick up on this and change my behavior. I didn't quite get it, though. And looking at my uncle now, I see him constantly looking for something to bring him some sort of inner peace or an answer to a question he can't even find the words to ask.

Over the years, I have become the Obi-Wan, Gandalf, and Dumbledore figure. There will be times I will get lost in thought, but I am thinking about solutions to problems. It doesn't mean that I do not still stumble and fall from time to time, but I do look for productive ways to handle the negative behaviors and to control them instead of giving in to them. Even when I was formally diagnosed with autism, I was never willing to let it be a crutch and to excuse the behavior. You can judge my success by my time as I worked at the university as a manager. I was a little bit older than the college students I was working with. They came to me for advice.

I worked with a guy who was getting upset. He had test anxiety and his grades were suffering. He got good grades in high school, so his parents thought he should be getting good grades in college. Out of his anger, he would hit himself or scald himself with hot water when he was in the shower. His girlfriend was also a friend of mine, but she couldn't get him to get professional help for what he was doing to himself. And some of the older ladies we worked with, who were more like a mother figure to him, couldn't get him to get help.

He came to me with his problems. I listened and told him my own struggles. I told him how I was seeing a psychiatrist. I told him seeing a doctor didn't make you weak, troubled, or an outcast. Sometimes we all need help in life. We should never be too proud to ask for help, or feel too isolated from other people to ask for help.

A couple of days later, his girlfriend comes up to me and thanks me. She said he was going to a doctor, which nobody else was able to get him to do, except for me. He also started to talk to his parents about what he was going through. They became more understanding.

As my nephews and niece are growing up, I have sometimes been called in to help out. I don't have children, and I am not trained in helping children. We were visiting my grandfather, who was in his 90s. My oldest nephew was in the back bedroom crying, even though he was a teenager. His parents talked to him, then they asked me to go talk to him. I asked him if he was okay. He said he didn't know why he was crying. I told him it was okay to cry. That is not something most people would tell a teenage boy, but it is the truth. Society just has the impression of what is right or wrong for some people to do. He came out of the bedroom a few minutes later and joined the rest of the family.

I do not claim to be perfect, but I made a decision a long time ago to not let my negative behaviors get the best of me. I could overcome them. I might make mistakes from time to time and give into my anger, but I don't have to turn into Darth Vader. I don't have to be trapped in the suit as a victim from the choices I have made in life. I can remain the good man, who will occasionally stumble and fall.

My mom doesn't like that I call myself autistic because I'm not as autistic as other people. She thinks they have really severe behavioral problems. The difference is that I grew up thinking I was normal. These other people grew up with the label. If you think you child will never achieve much, you will excuse the negative behavior and let the child get away with it. I'm not insulting anybody's parenting skills. I think you should encourage children to overcome the negative, which is harder to do if you think of autism as a disease or disability instead of a difference.

But you should also understand that autistic children might be more sensitive to their surroundings than other children. Think about the sensitivities in the same way you would an animal. We are learning that instead of being less sensitive to feelings that autistic people might actually be able to feel more and empathize more than neurotypical people. Animals can sense things like weather, emotions, and other things that humans cannot. What if the autistic person can do the same thing? What if they are becoming anxious because they can sense the parent is anxious trying to potty train them, or make them speak? The kid might be picking up on your frustrations and anxieties, which is going to make the activity you are trying to get them to do have more pressure on it than it already has.

And I'm not going to be apologizing to parents of autistic children or to autistic people who are wanting to use the autism as a crutch or to claim to be a victim. Yes, there are difficulties in autism, but if you think everything is impossible, then it will be impossible. There is an Audrey Hepburn quote that has been circulating around the internet about how she hates the word "impossible" because the very word says, "I'm possible."

There is a great history of people with autism who have gone on to do amazing things. The only difference between them and autistic people today is that they didn't know they were autistic, so they didn't let a diagnosis stop them achieving what they wanted to do or from changing the world to fit their vision of what it should be.

Enable autistic children. Don't disable them. And I'm sorry, but I have been on autistic discussion boards. There are people on there that blame their lack of a job on their autism. They don't see their own negative attitude and victim mentality as part of the reason they don't get hired. We get back what we send out.

I have worked in the customer service industry for years. The customers that are nasty to me get the littlest amount of help I can give them. Sometimes I'm unable to do the return. They ones that treat me with respect and don't start yelling at me get a lot more help. They will sometimes get a refund and then something extra to make sure they return as a customer. I excuse the giving away of some additional food as great customer service, but it was really because they treated me with respect instead of treating me like an idiot.

There are lots of people with autism working in the Silicon Valley, but they don't know they have autism. It hasn't stopped them from getting jobs. And we can do all of the studies we want about people with autism and how many of them are unemployed, but the study will never look at their attitude. If you project negativity, you will get negativity back. Autism can only define you if you let it. I would rather define autism than to have it define me. Harness its benefits and overcome the weaknesses.

The A-Men

Some of you might be wondering why I called this book *The A-Men: Rethinking Autism*. Well, what if I could be like Professor Charles Xavier from *The X-men*? What if we stopped thinking about autism as a disease to be cured or a disability? What if it is human evolution that could bring about a better life for humanity?

Autism is on the rise, whether the rate of autism is actually increasing or our diagnosing of it is increasing. Autism seems to have always existed in human cultures. We have just thought the people were quirky and not disabled. The list of suspected autistics throughout history include Isaac Newton, Albert Einstein, Henry Ford, Thomas Edison, Michelangelo, Mozart, Jane Austen, Mark Twain, Hans Christian Andersen, Thomas Jefferson, Charles Darwin, and others who have made great contributions to society.

I don't think autism is new. Our awareness of it is. The incidences of autism might be on the rise, but we can't be sure of that. Our awareness has now made it easier for parents to get their children tested because they know the symptoms and signs.

And one of the reasons I don't like for it to be called a disease is that we might be trying to wipe out something because we are afraid of it instead of seeing how it can have an evolutionary advantage. I read an article the other day about a group of workers where everybody is normal, except for this one autistic person. As ideas are presented, the normal people look at the facts and will say that everything will work. Then the autistic person points out the flaw in the logic. The normal people re-examine the facts and discover the autistic person was right.

One of the advantages to being different is seeing the same problem in a different way. Considering how a significant portion of autistic people can excel at math and science naturally, we would be wiping out future advancements because somebody had the autistic label. Would you be willing to cure the next Einstein or Bill Gates? What great works of art would we also be destroying by trying to cure autism? Would we be wiping out the next Mozart or Michelangelo? Even in political theory, we need the next Thomas Jefferson to see that all men are created with inalienable rights.

Autism has been responsible for great advancements in our society. Being different and thinking differently has its benefits. We are constantly encouraging people to think outside the box. Autism does that naturally, but yet we fear it and want to cure it.

Some people have described forms of autism as being the only person in the story about the emperor's new clothes that realizes the emperor doesn't have new clothes. He's naked. The rest of society goes along with the idea that the emperor has new clothes.

Look at our society today. We have groups of people going along with the terrible treatment of other people, and nobody stands up and says that it is wrong. It is like people are afraid of being cast out from society. A girl can be drunk, gang raped, and videotaped during the entire process, and nobody near the situation puts an end to it. It's not like it is happening in private. It is happening in a public space and is a public spectacle, but the normal people are afraid of upsetting the social structure. But we are also spending more time teaching social skills today than we have in the past.

In England, there was a young gay man with Asperger's. On his 18th birthday, guests at his party wrote gay slurs on his body, covered him in oils, and then set him on fire. Again, this was in a public space and not in private where there were no witnesses. Why didn't somebody speak up?

There are times I will do unpopular things because I do not see the societal reasons behind it. I'm not going to do something I don't believe in just because everybody else is doing it. If somebody can't still be my friend for my morals and beliefs, then they are not really my friend in the first place. And if I see somebody being bullied or taken advantage of, I'm going to speak up about it. I don't care how rich or popular they are. Money and popularity do not give you an excuse to treat other people as inferior to you. Money comes and goes. I have seen poor people become rich and rich become poor. And popular people do not always stay popular.

And why do we have this idea that different is bad? Different is something that just isn't the same. It doesn't make it unequal or less than. Different can sometimes be better than something that is the same.

Our focus has been on what autism can't do. Nobody seems to think about what autism can do. Autistic people have made great advances in math, science, the arts, and politics. I consider this a good thing that was brought about by people looking at the world differently.

I'm not going to say that autism is the greatest thing in the world. I have meltdowns. I feel like I don't belong most of the time. I don't have that many friends. I don't understand romantic relationships. If I'm ever going to get married, I will need to find a woman who can walk me through the beginning of a relationship. I am one of the few men in the world who can be trained.

And for all of these disadvantages, there are things I excel at that I don't know how to explain to other people. When I released my first novel, the first professional review I received had me being compared to J.D. Salinger, except better. They were proclaiming me the future of literature. This couple read it, then they shared it with one of their sisters who has several degrees. It became something they just had to share. I would then get e-mails from young aspiring authors wanting advice from me on how to become a successful author. I didn't know what to tell them. I taught myself how to write by watching movies and spending my free time writing, reading what I had written, and rewriting what I had written. I was never formally trained.

Instead of socializing with kids my own age, I spent my high school years writing and revising my books. That is how I make part of my money. In a couple of years, I should be able to make some really decent money from my book sales. But I will be making this money because of my odd, anti-social behavior I exhibited in high school.

After I was becoming more successful as an author, I did take a grad class in creative writing. I was in there with people who actually had degrees in creative writing. They were continuing their education. I was basically starting mine. I was amazed at how terrible their writing was, though.

I've learned over the years from the reception of my writing that I don't know what to tell people about becoming an author. I'm different because I'm autistic. Some people are calling me a genius because of this. Others don't like me for being different. My books have never gotten middle of the road reviews. I have either made people love me or hate me. I'm talking I get either 4 and 5 star reviews or 1 and 2 star reviews.

In college, I got a degree in Art History because it was easy for me to memorize artists, titles, and dates. Other people struggled with this. Now that I now I am autistic, I understand why it was easy for me. Not only can I memorize easily, but I can notice patterns in things, which helped with the Art History essays and papers.

I guess the question is if I were offered the opportunity to not be autistic, would I decide to be cured?

I guess the only way I can answer that is with the same answer I gave to somebody I worked with when they asked me, "If you could be somebody else, who would you be?" I said, "I would be myself. I'm happy being myself.

Even though I might think I would like somebody else's life, there would be hidden things about it that might be worse than what I currently have."

You see, when I was growing up, I spent a lot of time with the Muppets. Some of the things that stuck with me the most was Kermit singing "Bein' Green." Being autistic has its problems. I might think it might be better to be something else. "When autistic is all there is to be, it could make you wonder why? But why wonder? Why wonder? I am autistic and it'll do fine. It's beautiful, and I think it's what I want to be."

The other thing I learned was from a song Gonzo sang. It's called "The Wishing Song." It's about wishing you had different things in life, including being somebody other than yourself. Then somebody tells him they like him the way he is. The rest of the song is about the things he does have and he is happy to be himself.

I'm not going to tell you autism is the most wonderful thing in the world. But it also isn't the worst thing in the world to be either. We all have strengths and weaknesses. We all need help as we go through this life. What difference does it make if my help happens to be with social skills or other autism related issues?

Instead of feeling sorry for myself, I would rather look at all of the things I can do. I just wonder what other autistic people could achieve if we would change our focus from them being disabled to being abled with some difficulties and areas in which they need help.